Balcony Women

An Inspirational
Small Group Guide
for Widows

Balcony Women™
Lifting Each Other Up In Love

"Therefore, encourage and build each other up."
1 Thessalonians 5:11

www.balconywomen.com

Balcony Women
An Inspirational Small Group Guide for Widows

Copyright 2022 by Melissa Phenicie.

Published by Design Vault Press, LLC
www.designvaultpress.com

First Edition: May, 2022
ISBN: 978-1-7351818-3-7

Balcony Women ™
Lifting Each Other Up In Love

What is a Balcony Woman?

A Balcony Woman is a woman God places in your life to encourage you. You will find her in the balcony of your life, hanging over the railing cheering you on. She is a woman who genuinely wants to see you succeed and is excited when good things happen to you.

Our nonprofit was formed to lift up, support and love the precious women in our communities. Proceeds from our online sales and nonprofit donations fund two widow dinners each year, host monthly widow support groups, furnish volunteer opportunities, provide encouragement and education, and fund small group curriculum for women of all ages with the goal of establishing supportive communities who will, in turn, fulfill God's calling to support the widows in their communities.

Learn more at www.balconywomen.com. Text "Balcony Women" to (202) 858-1233 or scan our code to donate.

*I*n the Bible, the feather represents care, love and protection.

Just as a bird soaring through the sky can view things from a higher perspective, the feather symbolizes the ability to see a bigger picture and understand what is important to focus on.

GOD.

"He will cover you with His feathers, and under His wings you will find refuge; His faithfulness will be your shield and rampart."
Psalms 91:4 (NIV)

Small Group Guide

Widows don't typically like to discuss their pain and try to cover it up. It's devastating to us. When we are able to discuss our hurts, great healing comes about, as well as freedom from the pain. You make friends with other widows and have fun. You find that you can share experiences that you can't share with anyone else.

Our purpose in creating this guide is to help widow groups of all sizes conduct their meetings or help a widow on her grief journey when no widow support group is available. There is no directing, counseling, steering toward a predetermined goal, no manipulation, no "fixing" — just a complete reliance on God to work.

Our guide is divided into 12 sections, one for each monthly meeting. Each section has an opening prayer, widow voices, widow stories, Bible verses, a notes section, and a closing prayer.

Have questions? Reach out to us via the Contact page on our website, www.balconywomen.com.

Joy Journal

In addition to the small group guide, we have found it helpful for widows to utilize a Joy Journal. This is a simple tool to help you focus on positive events of the day.

Start by writing one positive thing that happens each day in your journal before you go to bed. It doesn't have to be a momentous event. It can be, "I brushed my teeth today." The purpose of this tool is to focus on the good God is doing in your life. Start by listing one, then two, and gradually progress to add more and more. Soon, finding joyful moments becomes a positive habit. You will find yourself looking for the good in each day so that you will have content for your journal.

We encourage you to write Bible verses that speak to you, God Sightings you experience, and tools you have learned in your journal, too.

The journal is a useful tool when you experience a grief trigger and are struggling. You can review your entries to see the progress you have made, be reminded of the God Sightings on your journey, and find tools to help you.

Joy Journals are private and aren't meant to be shared in the group unless you feel prompted.

5–Step Meeting Agenda

1. **Prayer:** The opening prayer serves to create an atmosphere in which the Holy Spirit is welcomed to direct all conversations and actions. He is the healer and restorer of the soul.
2. **Prayer Requests/God Sightings:** Volunteers from the group will share where they need to see God or where God is moving in their lives.
3. **Present the meeting Widow Voice Stories from the guide.** Each section has four related support material pages and an opportunity to take notes.
4. **Healthy Discussion:** Widows share their thoughts concerning meeting the needs of their group members by sharing their faith and ideas. This should be a safe place for each member to feel free to cry, laugh, be angry, joyful. Each meeting is a place for transparency, authenticity, and confidentiality. No judgment.
5. **Pray.**

Sample Meeting Outline

- Start the meeting with an opening prayer.
- Ask the ladies if they have any prayer requests/God Sightings that relate to their grief journey.
- Remind them to choose a verse to focus on for the month. Go over the verses provided to help them get started.
- Read the "Widow Voices" and see if they can relate to any of them. This is a great opportunity to find tools to help them on their journey. If someone can relate, ask how they handled a particular situation. Their journey may help others.
- Use the widow stories as discussion starters. You may not get to all the stories, depending on the needs presented, or you may need more. You can find additional resources on our Balcony Women for Widows private Facebook page.
- Let the group know of upcoming special/trigger dates from the roster so that they remember to encourage each other during the month.
- Close in prayer.
- Meetings normally last one hour.

Leader Suggestions

- Make sure every widow has access to a Joy Journal and encourage them to add content every day. Journals are private and not meant to be shared in the group unless a widow feels led to share an experience.
- Encourage widows to choose a Bible verse to focus on for the month and write it in their Joy Journals. We have included verse ideas in each section.
- Keep the meetings focused on finding tools to help widows on their grief journey. NO political discussions, NO gossip, NO outside stories.
- ANYTHING shared at the group meeting MUST stay in the group meeting unless permission has been granted to share.
- Encourage the ladies to meet outside your regular meeting for fellowship and bonding. Go to lunch, have coffee, or go to an event.
- Create a group roster as a way for the ladies to reach out and support each other between meetings. Include special dates such as birthdays, anniversaries, husband's birthday, and his heavenly birthday.
- Assign leadership roles within the group. Example roles:
  - **Leader**: Facilitates meetings.
  - **Roster**: Compiles and updates roster.

- **Communications**: Reminds group of meetings.
- **Special Needs**: Organizes dinners or other needs during times such as surgeries, illnesses, loss, et cetera.

All content in this guide was created by widows for widows. Our hope is to produce a new guide each year. If you have a prayer, Bible verse and commentary, and/or story you would like to contribute to the next edition, please email it to Melissa@balconywomen.com. We will protect your identity. We request that if you use actual people in your story, please change their names.

Table of Contents

Fear

Meeting Opening Prayer

Dear Lord, I am afraid. I don't know what is going to happen next in my life. I need You now and need to feel Your presence more than ever. I need You to assure me that You are in control. Please remind me day by day, hour by hour, and sometimes second by second that You are near. I am laying my fear at Your feet. Please guide me through my fears and remind me that I can trust in You. I know I can't do this on my own. I need you, Lord.

Widow Voices

- Making decisions on my own has become fearful to me as a widow.
- I didn't know who to call when the water heater started to leak.
- I fear being alone as I get older.
- I fear new experiences and the unknown.
- I fear financial instability. How will I take care of myself?
- I fear coming home to an empty house.

Scripture Focus

1

"I sought the LORD, and he answered me; he delivered me from all my fears. Those who look to him are radiant; their faces are never covered with shame.
The angel of the LORD encamps around those who fear him,
and he delivers them."
Psalms 34:4-5,7 (NIV)

David models what we can do when we are afraid, and he shows us how God responds. David gives us a "front row seat" to what it is like to depend on God in our darkest hour.

Widow Story

"Who's afraid of the Big Bad Mail? Me! Each time I reach into the mailbox I cringe, wondering what will be in there. Paperwork I don't understand or know what to do with, a bill that I may not be able to afford for a service I think I need, or another person wanting me to provide a death certificate, documented statement, signature or verification to prove that I am me and that I am the successor trustee. Who knew that paper could cause such anxiety? I am learning so much, and yet each step leads to yet another door to walk through. Since I no longer have my husband to help make decisions, I have to ...

Dare to ask!

People are amazingly helpful when you are honest and humble enough to admit, "I don't know what this is or what in the world I am supposed to do with it!" Job was right ... "But ask those who have been around, and they will tell you the truth." (Job 21:29 NLT)

Scripture Focus

2

"So do not fear, for I am with you; do not be dismayed, for I am your God. I will strengthen you and help you; I will uphold you with my righteous right hand."
Isaiah 41:10 (NIV)

God is always with us. He is with you day and night, no matter what you're going through. That's a promise! God promises to provide us with strength, and with help. When you're feeling like you can't go on, or you just don't know how you're going to get through the day, God will be right there with you to provide the strength and help you need.

Widow Story

"Widowhood brings with it fear and uncertainty. I have to remind myself the spirit of fear is NOT from God. The Holy Spirit lives in me and He is my helper. I am NOT alone. God promises to never leave us. I put my faith in Him and not in the world. I calm my fears by spending more and more time with God. I read my Bible, devotionals, and other uplifting materials.

I try to focus on today and what God has planned just for today. This keeps me from becoming overwhelmed. I believe God wants me to be happy and joyful. I purposely count my blessings each day in a joy journal. Even in grief, we are blessed in so many ways. We need to focus on the blessings and keep our eyes on God.

Scripture Focus

3

"Do not be afraid, only believe."
Mark 5:36 (NAS)

Often circumstances can begin to overwhelm belief, but this passage shows us that we need to keep God in focus because nothing is impossible with Him.

Widow Story

" Fear can be debilitating.

It can come and go. Fear never follows a predictable schedule, so I have to brace myself and stay in prayer to focus on God's truth when fear shows up.

I have learned that fear can also be an opportunity to learn and grow. Joy can be found on the other side of fear but sometimes that joy is a matter of choosing to see God's perspective.

I am trying to choose not to be afraid and instead believe that God has a plan and a purpose for me that will bring me joy.

Scripture Focus

4

*"Do not fear, for I have redeemed you; I have
summoned you by name; you are mine.
When you pass through the waters, I will be
with you; and when you pass through the
rivers, they will not sweep over you. When
you walk through the fire, you will not be
burned; the flames will not set you ablaze. For
I am the LORD your God."*
Isaiah 43:1-3 (NIV)

This is a command, accompanied by promises. By outward
circumstances, the people of Judah had reason to be
afraid of Babylon's army and exile. God points them past the
present circumstances to both this command and promise.

Widow Story

"As a widow, I struggle with finances. One Saturday I was really hungry for ham salad, but I told myself, "You don't need that." However, the sense that it was important for me to go to the grocery store was strong. I know it sounds silly, but I felt like I was supposed to buy ham salad. I went to the store, picked up the ham salad and placed it in my cart. As I walked up and down the aisles, I found other items I needed that happened to be on sale. At the checkout, I realized I had saved over twenty dollars due to the unknown bargains I happened upon.

In my heart, I felt that was God's way of showing He would provide and take care of my needs. God takes care of His widows. I do not need to be afraid or concerned. He will provide.

Fear: Reflection

_____

_____

_____

_____

_____

_____

_____

_____

_____

_____

_____

_____

_____

_____

_____

_____

_____

_____

_____

_____

_____

_____

_____

_____

_____

_____

_____

_____

_____

_____

_____

_____

_____

_____

_____

Dear God, Thank you for your perfect love.
May I walk in faith with you today.
In Jesus' name, Amen.

Assurance

Meeting Opening Prayer

*D*ear God, life isn't how I thought it would be. Everything seems to be in constant flux. Forgive me for feeling (and sometimes acting) like a toddler ... wanting my way, my plan, my husband and best friend. Help me to remember that, although I may not always understand why things happen as they do, that You, Mighty God, are ever faithful and unchanging. Your plans are better than my plans, and You will care for me always. Thank you for your patience and love. In Jesus' name I pray, Amen.

Widow Voices

- Spending time with other widows has helped me navigate grief.
- My faith, and knowing that my husband is spending eternity in heaven, gives me assurance.
- I am blessed with spiritual and emotional support from my family and friends.
- Spending time in prayer helps me; I know that my strength will come from the Lord.
- Grief support groups and counseling help me know that I am not losing my mind.
- Staying active and connected to others helps me persevere through the difficult days.

Scripture Focus

1

'"For I know the plans I have for you," de-
*clares the L*ORD, *"plans to prosper you and*
not to harm you, plans to give you hope and
a future. Then you will call on me and come
and pray to me, and I will listen to you. You
will seek me and find me when you seek me
with all your heart."'
Jeremiah 29:11-13 (NIV)

We spend time and waste energy trying to figure out how to get back to normal. God is with us no matter where we are. There is a great potential for good, for a future and hope, if we choose to embrace His presence. When the time comes to move, God will show us the way and the time.

Widow Story

"My friend Linda's husband died unexpectedly within weeks of my husband's death. She texted me early one morning to share that sad news and what began with a text has become a lifeline — an alarm clock to begin the day as we text each other between 6 and 7 every morning. Our content usually covers the agenda for the day, a new recipe, the mention of challenges and small victories in our journeys ... the mundane "normal" so lacking in my world. This fellow widow can read my whining or fear between the lines and knows when I need encouragement or a kick in the seat of the pants.

Between 9 and 10 p.m., the ritual repeats itself: a report about our day — the good, the bad, the authentic reality. Never once has either of us sought advice (although we would each be glad to give or receive it); we just seek connection. This is a lifeline that is more important than I could have ever predicted — a God gift that neither of us saw coming: the human assurance that we're not walking on this path alone.

Scripture Focus

2

*"You have searched me, L<small>ORD</small>, and you
know me. You know when I sit and when I
rise; you perceive my thoughts from afar. You
discern my going out and my lying down; you
are familiar with all my ways."*
Psalms 139:1-3 (NIV)

Have you ever wondered if God sees and knows you individually? Does He care about you? This psalm resoundingly tells us, "Yes! God knows me." Not only does the God of the Bible know of you in general, He knows you personally.

Widow Story

66 The Word of God is filled with promises from God that I am not alone. Reading my Bible daily and keeping those promises on my lips and in my heart assures me that even when I sleep, cry, become angry or wail in despair, God sees me. He knows. He cares. He will take care of me. He has a plan.

"Nothing can ever separate
us from God's love."
Romans 8:38 (NLT)

As a widow, I am not set aside — even though it can feel that way. I have a purpose! I have protection! I have God!

Scripture Focus

3

*"Now faith is the assurance of things hoped
for, the conviction of things not seen."*
Hebrews 11:1 (ESV)

A living faith in God's Word and the confident hope in His promises are two graces that embrace each other in love at the foot of the Cross.

Widow Story

"I have learned that God will show up. Through the loss of my husband, when breast cancer struck, in selling "our" home, in finding "my" home, in dealing with the big and small decisions of living by myself.

In each of these situations, God met my needs and carried me forward. My goal is to wholly depend on God all the time, not just when I am in *widow crisis* mode.

I take it one day a time. I take a deep breath and tell myself I will trust God; I will remember He has a plan. He knows the gophers have returned to my yard; he knows the door frame is warped. Everything will be okay. He will guide me to respond as I need to. Just for today, I will breathe and believe.

Scripture Focus

4

*"... and hope does not disappoint, because
the love of God has been poured out within
our hearts through the Holy Spirit who was
given to us."*
Romans 5:5 (NAS)

Hope is founded in God's trustworthy goodness and the gracious promises of our Heavenly Father. Hope is centered on the never-failing Word of God and His many precious promises.

Widow Story

"Fearful that I was losing my mind, I reluctantly spoke up at a widow support group meeting. I'd been placing a pillow on my husband's side of the bed each night. It helped me fall asleep. I knew he was no longer there, but I just needed something there in his place.

When I told my group, many confessed that they did the same thing. It was such a relief to know I was not alone. They gave me assurance that I was not losing my mind.

Widows need other widows. No one can understand this journey unless they have been through it.

Assurance: Reflection

_____

_____

_____

_____

_____

_____

_____

_____

_____

_____

_____

_____

_____

_____

_____

_____

Dear Father, When I am afraid, remind me of
your presence and your love. In Jesus' name,
Amen.

Peace

Meeting Opening Prayer

*H*eavenly Father, peace eludes me. I want it. I know You offer it, and all I have to do is claim it. But I am afraid. I am afraid to "be still," afraid that the reality of life as a widow will swallow me; I'm insecure in my ability to discern your voice. Help me, Father, to claim your gift of peace, purchased with the sacrifice of Jesus. I have nothing to fear, for You are all I need. In the name of Jesus I pray, Amen.

Widow Voices

- Knowing my husband loved me gives me peace.
- Sometimes, calling Jesus by name is all I can do.
- Knowing I will see my loved one again in heaven helps me get through each day.
- I tell myself, "I can do all things through Christ."
- Being a part of a community gives me peace.
- I journal to give me peace.
- I like to relive my memories.
- Believing the promises of God settles my aching heart.

Scripture Focus

1

"I will lie down and sleep in peace, for you alone, O Lord, make me dwell in safety."
Psalms 4:8 (NIV)

David enjoyed such a close relationship with God that he was able to get a good night's rest. He trusted the Lord to keep him safe. Instead of tossing and turning at night, he tossed his burdens onto the Lord's shoulders and turned his troubles over to Him.

Widow Story

"I miss so much about my husband ... the pinch on my butt as he walked by me, the love notes he was notorious for, even his snoring (which had me considering separate houses) and the "bargains" he could not resist — even if we did not use or need the product. But the tear-producing events are more likely to be the unexpected finding of Cheerios (Hubby's favorite snack) in the pocket of his old red hoody, having to purchase my own razors after almost 38 years because the ones I always borrowed from my husband's shaving kit are no longer there, even finding toilet paper on the roller. For all the years of our married life, I was the one who always replaced the empty roll. What I wouldn't give to find one of those empty toilet paper rolls, to hear his afternoon-nap snoring, to find smears of "something" across the kitchen counter after he had made a sandwich, to hear the theme song from "Jeopardy" or "American Pickers!"

When we stop obsessing about what we want, only then can we find what we need. Peace is promised by our Heavenly Father, and we can read Jesus' words in scripture, over and over again, reminding us that all we have to do is claim that peace we so desperately need and want. I am putting that on my daily to-do list!

Scripture Focus

2

"Peace I leave with you; my peace I give to
you; not as the world gives do I give to you.
Let not your hearts be troubled, neither let
them be afraid."
John 14:27 (ESV)

*D*on't be scared of your emotions. Let your sorrow wash over you, and give in to your feelings. Tears are healing. God is guiding you in your grief.

Widow Story

"All I want to do was sleep. I can't get to sleep. I can't stay asleep. Which is it? It is all of the above! Listening to music helps some widows. Reading helps other widows. As for me, I talk to God. I list in my mind all the times He has been faithful to me. I thank Him. I lay my worries at His feet. Often, taking that weight off my shoulders is enough to ease me into much needed sleep.

Taking care of my health — physical, spiritual, and emotional — depends upon having peace. God is waiting to give peace. I just need to remember to ask.

Scripture Focus

3

*"Come to me, all you who are weary and
burdened, and I will give you rest. Take my
yoke upon you and learn from me, for I am
gentle and humble in heart, and you will find
rest for your souls. For my yoke is easy and
my burden light."*
Matthew 11:28-30 (NIV)

Because our burdens are not simple, they are not relieved by simplistic platitudes. But a simple promise can relieve a complex burden, provided we believe that the power behind the promise is complex and strong enough to relieve our heaviness.

Widow Story

"I have had to learn that having peace does not mean I won't have a clogged brain, thinning hair, higher utility bills; that I won't cry unexpectedly, ache with loneliness, feel a bit envious of my friend leaving on a vacation with her husband.

It does mean that God will dry my tears, guide my actions, and protect me. He will stay with me on this rollercoaster ride of widowhood. He will forgive me and love me.

Scripture Focus

4

*"Rejoice in the Lord always. I will say it again:
Rejoice! Let your gentleness be evident to
all. The Lord is near. Do not be anxious about
anything, but in everything, by prayer and
petition, with thanksgiving, present your requests to God. And the peace of God, which
transcends all understanding, will guard your
hearts and your minds in Christ Jesus."*
Philippians 4:4-7 (NIV)

Joy is an attitude. And if it's an attitude, then joy is a choice. What the Holy Spirit is telling us is that we have a lot of control over our lives. It just isn't in the way we think. See the joy. Focus on the positives! Find the peace the Lord offers you.

Widow Story

"I often struggle to find peace. I know peace comes from God, but it is like my heart and mind have forgotten everything I learned as a young girl. All I can see are the losses I am experiencing. The loss of my husband, the loss of income, the loss of my friendships, the loss of my confidence, the list goes on.

I struggle to remember all the times God has been faithful, good and kind. I now intentionally look for ways God is moving in my ordinary daily life. Faith does not insulate us from struggles.

Grief is a reality that our Savior is personally acquainted with. Knowing this gives me some peace, even when grief exists in my daily life.

Peace: Reflection

_____
_____
_____
_____
_____
_____
_____
_____
_____
_____
_____
_____
_____
_____
_____
_____
_____
_____
_____

_____

_____

_____

_____

_____

_____

_____

_____

_____

_____

_____

_____

_____

_____

_____

_____

_____

_____

_____

*Dear Lord, thank you for caring for me today,
tomorrow and every day. I ask for peace to
put aside all the anxious thoughts. In Jesus'
name, Amen.*

Strength

Meeting Opening Prayer

God, we are assured that your grace is always available to us and sufficient for our needs. I need strength, Father, for the ability to let go of what has been so that I can receive what You want to give me. Some days I need strength to simply get out of bed, complete another form, face another evening alone. I need strength, Father — all day, every day. Thank you that I can rest assured You will meet me wherever I am. In Jesus' name I pray, Amen.

Widow Voices

- I need strength to deal with my loneliness.
- I am finding it hard to build a new life.
- Managing my home is proving to be difficult by myself.
- I don't feel like I fit in anymore.
- I am doing my best to set a good example for my family.
- I have trouble finding my purpose.
- I need strength to move forward.
- I find it hard to just get up and act normal.

Scripture Focus

1

*"What is impossible with man is possible with
God."*
Luke 18:27 (NIV)

Many things are hard for us. Others seem impossible. Jesus wants us to realize that when we live for the Kingdom, if we trust in God's power to be at work within us, then we can do far more than we would ever imagine possible.

Widow Story

"Fatigue like I have never experienced ... I can't seem to sleep it away, exercise it into history, nourish it enough with a healthy diet so that it leaves me alone ... and I sure can't ignore it. There are days when all I want to do is sit. On those days, my brain is mush. Holding a thought long enough to execute it is almost impossible. My mind and body are exhausted from two years of overload ... with no co-pilot to help navigate, no partner to share the burdens, no hubby to defend and protect me against critics, nobody to play point/counterpoint when a big decision needs to be made, no superhero to rescue me if I screw up, no taster to tell me if the casserole needs more salt, no admirer to notice how I look and make me smile by saying, "You look cute!" It's all on me! Mess up? Got to figure out how to fix it. Get it right? Nobody to celebrate with me.

Distractions are constant. There is always something else that needs to be done, something else to be decided, something else to worry about. Distractions cause "do-overs," and "do-overs" are exhausting. Jesus was very clear in the answer for "this": "Come to me and I will give you rest." Give yourself grace. Be okay and embrace your "no" not as laziness but as a posture of grace. Honor your own capacity at this moment in time. *Listen! Obey! Trust!*

Scripture Focus

2

*"I love you, O Lord, my strength. The Lord is
my rock, my fortress and my deliverer; my
God is my rock, in whom I take refuge. He is
my shield and the horn of my salvation, my
stronghold. I call to the Lord, who is worthy
of praise, and I am saved from my enemies."*
Psalms 18:1-3 (NIV)

David penned this song of deliverance to the Lord on the day He rescued him from the hand of his enemies. David was a man after God's own heart who not only made the claim above because of his head knowledge, but due to an inner experience of the heart.

Widow Story

" Sometimes I struggle to believe that God can give me strength. It's like my heart and mind have amnesia. As a widow, I feel the weight of losing the life I had planned and the secondary losses that come with the loss, and it suppresses all the memories of when Jesus has helped me.

I don't want to be like Thomas in John 20:25; He had witnessed Jesus' miracles, yet it's like he forgot who he knew Jesus to be.

God has strength for you and me, even when we have amnesia. He doesn't judge us when our faith wavers. It helps me if I look for Him as He is moving, even in my ordinary days. I look for evidence that He is with me and is at work, no matter what doubt tries to say. I write what I see in my Joy Journal to help remind me when I have amnesia.

Scripture Focus

3

*"Do you not know? Have you not heard? The
Lord is the everlasting God, the Creator of
the ends of the earth. He does not faint or
grow weary; His understanding is unsearch-
able. He gives power to the faint and to him
who has no might he increases strength.
Even youths shall faint and be weary and
young men shall fall exhausted; But they who
wait for the LORD shall renew their strength;
They shall mount up with wings like eagles;
They shall run and not be weary; They shall
walk and not faint."*
Isaiah 40:28-31 (ESV)

God is not too weak to act on your behalf, nor is fatigue an obstacle for the Creator in caring for you.

Widow Story

"I don't feel like I fit in anywhere. It's like I'm at a dinner party for six, and I am number seven. I don't really belong in the couples' class at church, and I don't want to be in the singles' class.

I feel like an outsider. Everyone else is going about their normal lives ... and mine has stopped. It's like my family and friends have just erased my husband and now tell me it is time to move on.

The best thing I did for myself was finding a widow community. It is a place where I fit in and can share my grief journey with others who "get it." We may be on different paths, but the journey is the same. We gain strength from each other, and God.

Scripture Focus

4

*"I can do all things through Christ who gives
me strength."*
Philippians 4:13 (NIV)

*D*o all things" does not mean "achieve all things," but instead promises that we are strong because of what Jesus provides. We can endure all things, good or bad, *through Christ.*

Widow Story

" **A**cceptance of a profound loss comes in fits and starts. Perhaps it is when you gaze at your husband's name chiseled into a block of cold granite for the hundredth time. Or when you cross the room to sit in his chair because that is easier than seeing it empty.

For me, it came late one night when I placed a bookmark at the end of a chapter, then gently closed the current novel in my hands and switched off the light.

Reading aloud to my husband in bed was a habit of many years. Discussions over the latest twists and turns in the story plot always followed, at least until he fell asleep.

Recently, keeping silent counsel on the just-read pages, I realized that life is like a novel laid out in chapters with a beginning, middle and end. And, although a beloved character is missing in my life, I am girded with God's promised strength. Tomorrow, I begin a new chapter in the continuing story of me.

The last page has not been turned.

Strength: Reflection

_____

_____

_____

_____

_____

_____

_____

_____

_____

_____

_____

_____

_____

_____

_____

_____

_____

_____

_____

_____

_____

_____

_____

_____

_____

_____

_____

_____

_____

_____

_____

_____

_____

_____

_____

Give me, and those I love, perseverance and patience during our time of need. In Jesus' name, Amen.

Grace

Meeting Opening Prayer

God of grace. Thank you for the grace so many have showered on me — my family, friends, co-workers, and even the stranger in the Costco parking lot who loaded a case of water bottles into my car. Your grace, Father, is boundless! The deeper my need, the greater Your grace is! Help me to receive the gift of grace with a grateful and loving spirit and to give grace to others with that same gratitude and love. I ask this in my Savior's name, Amen.

Widow Voices

- I have chosen to give grace to my family and friends, who don't understand my grief.
- I believe grace is the power given us as a gift to accomplish the will of God in our lives as we grieve.
- God is giving me the assurance that everything will work out.
- I live by the verse, "My grace is sufficient for you." (2 Corinthians 12:9 NIV)
- God's grace has been amazing. He listens to me praise Him, but understands how sad I am at times, and blesses me with good memories.

Scripture Focus

1

*"And we know that God causes everything
to work together for the good of those who
love God and are called according to his
purpose for them."*
Romans 8:28 (NIV)

All things are not good. God takes things that are, in
and of themselves, devastating and unwanted and puts
them together to provide healing.

Widow Story

"Waste not, want not." I am sure when my grandmother said those words, she had no idea I would apply that lesson as my rationale for eating cheese nachos for breakfast or making a half gallon of ice cream covered in chocolate syrup disappear — each a response because I was having a "suck your thumb" kind of day. Heater not working on a cold winter day? Look in the fridge! Grace will find you ... even on those "suck your thumb" days. Maybe grace will come in a phone call or text from a friend, maybe in your daily devotional, or maybe in the realization that nobody will know about your breakfast choice unless you tell them! We widows stick together ... I won't tell if you won't!

Scripture Focus

2

*"My grace is sufficient for you, for my power
is made perfect in weakness."*
2 Corinthians 12:9 (NIV)

No matter what you and I are facing, and no matter what tests and trials we may be required to face, we have God's full assurance that His grace is sufficient for every eventuality that may come our way.

Widow Story

" No matter what you say or how hard you try to help others understand, they can't understand unless they have lived it.

Defending yourself against someone who cannot understand is a waste of your time and emotions.

My advice is to just give them grace. The important thing to remember is that everyone's grief journey is different. There is no right or wrong way to grieve.

I often need grace for things I have said or done, or for things I have failed to say or do. Give yourself and others grace. If you are progressing, no matter how slowly, then you are doing it right.

Scripture Focus

3

"Let us then with confidence draw near to the throne of grace, that we may receive mercy and find grace to help in time of need."
Hebrews 4:16 (ESV)

There may be many who are compassionate and wise who will give you a hug or share an encouraging word, but there is One who understands our needs. And He will respond with love and compassion. There is One with whom you can have that intimate talk, and there is One who knows your tears. God invites us. He gives us the right to come boldly.

Widow Story

"What is wrong with me? I was told I would go through five stages of grief (denial, anger, bargaining, depression, and acceptance) and then I would be okay. The five stages of grief don't seem to apply to me.

My stages of grief are overwhelming sadness, anger, guilt, loneliness, confusion, fear, and anxiety.

Our society doesn't know what to do with grief. We think it is something to get over, as if we can check each stage off and move on to the next one.

Whatever your stages of grief, you can find grace to help you on your journey when you draw near to God. It is normal to experience grief in different stages and in a different order than other widows.

Scripture Focus

4

*"But to each one of us grace has been given
as Christ apportioned it."*
Ephesians 4:7 (NIV)

God brings each person exactly what is needed, depending on who and where we are.

Widow Story

"My first thoughts as a widow often are not the best choices for responding to people who mean well but say things that hurt. They haven't lived my grief experience and can't possibly understand what I am enduring. I have learned they don't know what they don't know.

Someone wise suggested that I have prepared responses when someone utters a hurtful comment. I tend to use these responses: "Thank you for caring," or "I am blessed by the life we lived together."

It is useless to explain yourself to people who cannot understand your journey. The truth is we don't want them to have to understand. We wouldn't want anyone to grieve the loss of their spouse. Give grace, and hopefully you will be given grace in return.

Grace: Reflection

_____

_____

_____

_____

_____

_____

_____

_____

_____

_____

_____

_____

_____

_____

_____

_____

_____

_____

_____

_____

_____

_____

_____

_____

_____

_____

_____

_____

_____

_____

_____

_____

_____

_____

_____

_____

*Lord, I believe that you alone are able to help
me. Thank you for your unfailing mercy and
grace in my time of need. In Jesus' name,
Amen.*

Trust

Meeting Opening Prayer

Dear God, disappointment, fears, and uncertainty are all around. Intellectually, I know that change is part of life. But living in a constant state of change is entirely different; I can't seem to get my bearings. Just when I think I can breathe, another change smacks right into me. Thank you for being my anchor, the one and only, forever faithful, and unchanging God whom I can trust. "But You remain the same, and Your years will never end," says the psalmist. (Psalms 102:27 NIV) Thank you, Father. Grow my trust! In the name of Jesus I pray, Amen.

Widow Voices

- I have had to learn to trust God and His plan for my life.
- I have had to trust that God is in control.
- I have had to learn to trust myself in the decisions I now make on my own.
- I learned quickly that not all the people in my life are trustworthy.
- It is hard to trust when you are alone.
- I have learned who my real friends are and who I can trust with my doubts and sorrows.

Scripture Focus

1

*"Trust in the Lord with all your heart and lean
not on your own understanding; in all your
ways acknowledge him, and he will make
straight your paths."*
Proverbs 3:5-6 (ESV)

We may feel lost and confused as we grieve, but God has a plan for everything. He knows your journey and how to get you on a path of healing. Place your faith and trust in Him.

Widow Story

"I know that I can trust God. I know that I should — that HE IS ENOUGH! And I know that I am enough. Scripture promises that. So why is it so hard to trust this "widow" version of myself? Why does this once decisive, in-charge, professional now get nervous when faced with simple decisions? Why does Super Mom's cape get all twisted as she wonders, "Will I be able to … ?" "Can I take care of … ?" Like that elusive set of keys that always seems to hide when I need them most, trust is often just out of my reach. I know I have it; I just can't find it.

I read a great suggestion not long ago for "resetting" trust in yourself. On those days when I feel like I just don't have the "trust juice" needed to fulfill what life is requiring, I look at my track record. I have survived the last 26,280 days. I can trust myself to survive this day, too. God is trusting me with this day. I can trust me, too!

Scripture Focus

2

"Delight yourself also in the Lord, and He shall give you the desires of your heart. Commit your way to the Lord, trust in Him, and He shall bring it to pass. Cease from anger, and forsake wrath; do not fret. It only causes harm."
Psalms 37:4-5, 8 (NKJV)

This world can never satisfy our deepest longings, but if we choose to delight in God's way, He will always provide above and beyond our *expectations.*

Widow Story

"Before becoming a widow, I hated the word; I never associated it with grief and anger. I assumed there would be sadness, anxiety, and loneliness ... but not anger.

I found myself so angry at God for what I thought He'd allowed to happen to me. I was mad at the loss of the future my husband and I had planned. I was angry that I had to watch other married couples live their "happily ever after" after mine was taken from me.

He tells us to bring everything to Him in prayer. There were many nights spent on my knees, crying in anger to Him before I chose to stop with the anger and start delighting in Him again. Anger only made my grief worse. I needed to trust in Him and He has helped me find peace beyond my expectations.

Scripture Focus

3

"But blessed is the one who trusts in the Lord, whose confidence is in Him. They will be like a tree planted by the water that sends out its roots by the stream. It does not fear when heat comes; its leaves are always green. It has no worries in a year of drought and never fails to bear fruit."
Jeremiah 17:7-8 (NIV)

Trusting in the Lord is simply believing what God has said. It is having faith in the incarnate Word of God and trusting all that the Lord has revealed to us in the written Word of God. It pleases the very heart of God when His children depend on Him utterly and believe in His Word.

Widow Story

"*I* used to be a productive person. I was organized and able to get things done. I gauged the success of my day by the checked-off items on my to-do list. Now I feel so lost and unable to accomplish the simplest of tasks. Grief has changed my definition of a successful day.

Sometimes all I am able to do is breathe, so I make myself take deep breaths to calm my panic and the overwhelming emotions that hit me. I have learned that it is normal to feel this way, and that the wave will pass if I just breathe through it.

Just breathe in, breathe out and remember that moving forward and being productive on your grief journey means taking it one step at a time.

Scripture Focus

4

"Give all your worries and cares to God, for
He cares about you."
1 Peter 5:7 (NLT)

Strength will be freely given when we admit our weaknesses and inabilities, and we are charged to hand over all our cares and disappointments to the Lord. He has promised to bear all our burdens because of His loving kindness and tender mercy towards us.

Widow Story

"Trust is tough as a widow. Do I trust this vendor? Can I trust this advice? And strange as it seems, I also have trouble trusting myself. Did I make the right decision? Did I remember to lock the door?

I love having other widows in my life now. I need them. We help each other with recommendations, insights, observations, information and support. Don't try to navigate grief alone. This journey is so much easier when you have other widows walking alongside you.

Trust: Reflection

_____
_____
_____
_____
_____
_____
_____
_____
_____
_____
_____
_____
_____
_____
_____
_____
_____
_____
_____
_____
_____

– Trust –

_____
_____
_____
_____
_____
_____
_____
_____
_____
_____
_____
_____
_____
_____
_____

*Father, forgive me when my faith is weak. I
love you and believe that you are here with
me. In Jesus' name, Amen.*

Hope

Meeting Opening Prayer

*H*eavenly Father, thank you for those days when my cup is filled to the brim with hope ... for sunshine and smiles. Other days, I am left with an empty cup. On my "empty cup" days, thank you for always being available to refill my cup. All I have to do is ask. I am asking you now, God, to fill my cup once again with hope in You and your promises. In Jesus' name I pray, Amen.

Widow Voices

- I am still trying to find hope.
- I find hope in the little successes each day.
- Hope in grief is the hardest part.
- Knowing God is with me gives me hope.
- My hope lies in knowing I will see my husband again someday.
- Looking forward to a future gives me hope.
- Knowing it will get better provides me hope.
- The days I wake up stronger give me hope.

Scripture Focus

1

*"Blessed are you who weep now, for you shall
laugh."*
Luke 6:21 (NIV)

It may not feel like it now, but you will feel joy again. It
just takes time.

Widow Story

" *I* can't believe I still cry a lot at a song, a smell, a problem, when someone is unexpectedly nice or thoughtful. And I am not talking about a dainty tear in the eye. These unexpected tsunamis are makeup-spoiling, nose-running, hiccup-inducing displays of emotion that I can't predict or control. When the girls were babies, I wondered if I would ever be in public without a wet or sticky spot on my clothes. Now I wonder if I will get back home without a meltdown.

I often think of this advice: Pray the hardest when it is hardest to pray. As a widow, my everyday hopes are different. I am not hoping that my swimsuit from last year will still fit or that Hubby and I can I make a 7 p.m. movie, or that my pantry is stocked with the snacks we all love. I am now hoping the sprinkler system will work, that my bills won't continue to escalate while my income declines, that I can travel alone safely, that someone will sit by me in my new church, that my wonderful husband knew how much I loved him. My hope these days is also a renewed focus on my God — the Hope for all.

"Rejoice in our confident hope. Be patient in
trouble, and keep on praying."
(Romans 12:12 NLT)

Scripture Focus

2

*"May the God of hope fill you with all joy and
peace in believing, so that by the power of
the Holy Spirit you may abound in hope."*
Romans 15:13 (ESV)

By giving all our sorrow up to God, He can help us replace
the bad feelings with His joy, peace, and hope.

Widow Story

"*I* didn't know this was going to be so hard. There are days that I don't think I can do it anymore. My inability to move forward in a meaningful way has stolen my hope.

Recently I was told to look at my situation through God's eyes — to see my journey as an opportunity to trust God, and He will help me move forward in hope.

I began facing my fears through scripture. 2 Timothy 1:7 (NIV) has become my verse whenever the negative thoughts begin to overwhelm me. *"For the Spirit God gave us does not make us timid, but gives us power, love, and self-discipline."*

I choose to find my hope in God's word, and not in my ability to move forward by my own strength.

Scripture Focus

3

"Be joyful in hope, patient in affliction, faithful in prayer."
Romans 12:12 (NIV)

The power for hope, joy, patience, and faithfulness comes from the Holy Spirit. Pray faithfully to increase the hope that you have in Christ. Prayer will lead to patience and joy, even when we are being afflicted.

Widow Story

" The fear of the unknown tends to keep me stuck in my grief. Since becoming a widow, I find myself dealing with so many unknowns, and I no longer have a partner to help me work through problems.

I feel like the Israelites. Instead of looking at the land God was giving them, they let fear of the unknown overcome them.

I know hope is God's plan for His widows, but I will need to face my fears. I know I am not fearless, but I can *fear less*.

> *"Have I not commanded you to go? Be*
> *strong and courageous. Do not be afraid; do*
> *not be discouraged, for the Lord your God*
> *will be with you wherever you go."*
> Joshua 1:9 (NIV)

Scripture Focus

4

"Yes, my soul, find rest in God; my hope
comes from Him."
Psalm 62:5 (NIV)

Rather than worrying, we are to be still before the Lord. Rather than being anxious, we are to abide in Christ, and remain secure under the shadow of His wing. Our hope comes from Him alone.

Widow Story

"My husband went to be with the Lord seven years ago. Since then, I have gone through many different stages of grief. Expressed grief can be dealt with and released, but unresolved grief doesn't go anywhere. You must deal with it.

A friend sent me a bookmark entitled, "Praying God's Promises." It has been a blessing to me. One promise stated, "You will never leave nor forsake me because of the plans You have for my life." Jeremiah 29:11 (ESV) says, "'For I know the plans I have for you,' says the Lord, 'plans for welfare and not for calamity, to give you a future and a hope.'"

Trust God for your future. Hope in Him.

Hope: Reflection

_____
_____
_____
_____
_____
_____
_____
_____
_____
_____
_____
_____
_____
_____
_____
_____
_____
_____

_____

_____

_____

_____

_____

_____

_____

_____

_____

_____

_____

_____

_____

_____

_____

_____

_____

*My hope is in you, God, always
and forever! Amen.*

Faith

Meeting Opening Prayer

*H*ear my prayer, Father. I cannot imagine my journey without faith in your power and goodness. While days, nights, decisions, and circumstances are not easy, all is possible with You. Today I am just trying to breathe and survive, but my faith in You offers hope for days filled with peace and sweet memories. With your help, I can do this! Stay close, Lord. I need You. In gratitude and faith I pray, Amen.

Widow Voices

- I have had to have faith that I could care for myself.
- Having the faith that my husband is with Jesus has helped.
- I hang on to my faith in Jesus and my belief that all things are possible through Him.
- My faith tells me that there's more left for me to do here, or I wouldn't still be here.
- My faith is in a God that is so much bigger and more powerful than my grief, my fear, my lack of strength. He is my everything.
- I have had to have blind faith. I had no choice. I handed everything over to God.

Scripture Focus

1

"For we live by faith, not by sight."
2 Corinthians 5:7 (NIV)

Live and act in the belief and the Truth of the Word of God.

Widow Story

" A Melissa Radke story was shared on the April 14, 2020 podcast of Jen Hatmaker. This story tells of a grandpa and his young granddaughter, who were on the beach building sandcastles. Grandpa tells the child it is time to go home. The little girl sees the tide coming in and protests that the water will wash away all their beautiful sandcastles. That is indeed what happens, and the little girl is truly distressed. Grandpa takes her hand and assures her that it is okay. He tells her, "Those were castles for today. We can still make tomorrow's castles."

Well, I am not building castles ... maybe a lean-to on a good day. But God gets me on my feet every morning, and I am still standing. Perhaps there is a castle ahead.

"For I know the plans I have for you," says the Lord. "They are plans for good and not for disaster, to give you a future and a hope."
Jeremiah 29:11 (NLT)

Sounds like a castle to me.

Scripture Focus

2

"Even when we are too weak to have any faith left, He remains faithful and will help us, for He cannot disown us who are part of himself, and He will always carry out His promises to us."
2 Timothy 2:13 (TLB)

"Come to me, all you who are weary and burdened, and I will give you rest."
Matthew 11:28 (NIV)

Our faithfulness is sometimes dependent on our circumstances. God's faith is absolute, and He will always fulfill His promises.

In Christ, we can find rest from our weariness, burdens, and all that is weighing down on our hearts.

Widow Story

"Grief doesn't like to be ignored. I had to own it, wallow in it, scream at it, and — worst of all — acknowledge it. I finally realized that grief was not going to just go away, and that there is no quick fix to grief. I had to stop pretending it was not there. Grief stinks!

By ignoring it, I was making it worse. There will be days that are overwhelming and full of pain. With time, healing begins, and you will experience joy again. Although our hearts may still ache, joy is more powerful than grief. Allowing joy into our life doesn't mean that everything is wonderful. Our souls have the capacity to hold everything we need. There is room to carry heartache and joy.

Scripture Focus

3

*"Cast your cares on the Lord and He will
sustain you; He will never let the righteous be
shaken."*
Psalm 55:22 (NIV)

No matter what the cause of our cares and anxiety, God calls us to cast our cares upon Him. Whatever you are going through, it is not too much for God to bear. He doesn't just want your very great cares, but all of them.

Widow Story

"Grief made me feel like I was falling apart. I wanted to put all the pieces of me back together so I would be normal again.

I have learned that I don't get to go back to normal. I am not a puzzle — and even if I were, not all the pieces would fit now. Grief has changed me. I need to stop trying to make pieces fit that no longer serve me.

God has a purpose and a plan for my life. I need to let go of people and attitudes that don't fit anymore. It's excruciatingly hard to accept your new normal.

Staying in the heaviness of grief without allowing lightness in is an unhealthy way to live. Life will not be the same, but healing is possible, and living again is doable if you want it to be.

Scripture Focus

4

*"With man this is impossible, but not with
God; all things are possible with God."*
Matthew 19:26 (NIV)

It is an impossible task to live a Godly life in our own strength; it is only possible when we look to Him and rely on Him alone.

Widow Story

"If you want to be happy, you have to be happy on purpose. When you wake up, you can't just wait to see what kind of day you'll have. You have to decide what kind of day you will have.

Make purposeful choices each day. Do one thing that is hard. Do one thing that brings joy. Laugh. Rest. Exercise. Reflect. Learn. Pray. These are all steps that will keep you moving forward.

You can't fill the happiness void the same way you used to. You have to find new ways to find happiness. Things will never be the same, but different can be happy, too.

Faith: Reflection

_____
_____
_____
_____
_____
_____
_____
_____
_____
_____
_____
_____
_____
_____
_____
_____
_____
_____
_____
_____

_____

_____

_____

_____

_____

_____

_____

_____

_____

_____

_____

_____

_____

_____

_____

_____

*Lord God, help me to always remember that
nothing can separate me from your love. In
Jesus' name, Amen.*

Comfort

Meeting Opening Prayer

Dear God, my "person" — the one who held my hand, listened to me rant; the one who always had my back and even made a quick deposit into my account when I miscalculated the available balance — he is gone! But Father, You have always been and will always be the real source of my comfort, providing all I need. Sometimes that provision comes from You through our "person"; other times through a song, and often in the quiet of our special time with You. Thank you, Great Comforter, for all You do for me and for being (as Matthew West sings) "The God Who Stays." I love You. In my Savior's name I pray, Amen.

Widow Voices

- Taking baby steps and not doing everything at once gave me comfort.
- Finding peace in my new role has given me comfort.
- Finding my community of widows who understands and helps guide me has given me comfort.
- Learning new skills to take care of the things my husband used to take care of has given me comfort.
- My pets provide great comfort to me.
- Helping others gives me comfort and takes the focus off my grief.

Scripture Focus

1

*"The Lord is near to the brokenhearted and
saves the crushed in spirit."*
Psalms 34:18 (NIV)

Even if you feel alone, God is with you. In the moments you are having difficulty seeing Him, He is near. He is still watching over you.

Widow Story

"Who is *She*? Me, my body, my soul. That real person behind the smile and quick, "I'm fine!" answer to the well-intentioned question from friends and family: "How are you?" *She* knows I am not fine. Why else would my once thick and curly locks shed into the sink like a dog shedding its winter coat ... only to be replaced by thin and wispy strands? "You can't lie to your body," said the doctor kindly. *She* knows you are most certainly not fine. Arthritis arrived like a foreign terrorist; my once laser-like brain is scrambled by a lack of focus; memory leaks out my ears so that from opening the refrigerator door to scanning the shelves, the item sought will only be remembered after I leave the room. *She* wakes me in the middle of the night ... taunting me with mental and physical aches and pains, worries and sadness, reminding me that I am NOT FINE. I need a hug. I need a good cry. I need help with so many things. *She* candidly reminds me that I do need these things, but pride keeps me from asking for them from people who would certainly provide these things. How can others help if they do not know I need help because I am being dishonest and prideful? But *She* knows! "Need" is not a four-letter word ... well, it is — but not in a negative sense! *People cannot give you what they do not know you want or need.*

Scripture Focus

2

"Blessed be the God and Father of our Lord Jesus Christ, the Father of mercies and God of all comfort, who comforts us in all our affliction, so that we may be able to comfort those who are in any affliction, with the comfort with which we ourselves are comforted by God."
2 Corinthians 1:3-4 (ESV)

God comforts us in our grief, so we're able to have strength to give others help during their grief. We look to God as an example of how to provide comfort and love during times of sorrow.

Widow Story

"Widows need other widows.

I was talking to a sweet lady at church and inquired about a mutual friend that was just widowed. My friend's answer stopped me in my tracks. She said our widowed friend looked great; she was back at work and was smiling the last time she saw her. She said she was back to normal.

I knew there was no way to judge this widow by her outward appearance. Widows like to appear fine because we realize not everyone can handle our grief.

Grief doesn't just go away.

Scripture Focus

3

*"Blessed are those who mourn, for they shall
be comforted."*
Matthew 5:4 (ESV)

God will never abandon us during our grief. He will always provide us with love and hope.

Widow Story

"*I* know people mean well but sometimes they make such hurtful comments.

"Everything happens for a reason."

"He is in a better place."

"It is time to move on and get back to normal."

Or — my favorite — "I know exactly how you feel. My dog just died, and I am so sad."

I find no comfort in any of these comments. I have learned that comfort comes from God and other widows, who are the only ones that can truly understand.

For everyone else, I try to give them grace. They don't understand and will never understand until they experience it. I have created a standard response: "Thank you for caring," and smile, knowing they mean well.

Scripture Focus

4

*"He will wipe away every tear from their
eyes, and death shall be no more, neither
shall there be mourning, nor crying, nor pain
anymore, for the former things have passed
away."*
Revelations 21:4 (ESV)

In heaven, we will feel no pain, no sorrow, and there will be no death. Take heart. All of your grief will fall away, and you will only feel God's unending love.

Widow Story

" *E*veryone keeps telling me that time heals all wounds, but no one can tell me what I'm supposed to do *right now*.

Right now, I can't sleep. Right now, I can't eat. Right now, I still hear his voice and sense his presence even though I know he's not here. Right now, all I seem to do is cry.

I know all about time and wounds healing, but even if I had all the time in the world, I still don't know what to do with all this hurt *right now*.

Comfort: Reflection

_____

_____

_____

_____

_____

_____

_____

_____

_____

_____

_____

_____

_____

_____

_____

_____

_____

_____

_____

_____

_____

_____
_____
_____
_____
_____
_____
_____
_____
_____
_____
_____
_____
_____
_____
_____
_____

*Heavenly Father, help me to remember you
are the God of all comfort, all compassion.
Thank you for hearing my call for help. In
Jesus' name, Amen.*

Worry

Meeting Opening Prayer

*H*eavenly Father, worry consumes me. Like a thief, worry robs me of the rest, peace, joy, and confidence that You promise to all who place their trust in You. Help me, Father, to remember that the answer to every "what if?" is already known by You. You are bigger than any problem I might face. I am never alone. Thank you for that great gift! In your Son's name I pray, Amen.

Widow Voices

- I worry about taking care of my home and yard by myself.
- I worry about the unknown.
- I worry about my finances, but I know God will provide.
- I worry about making decisions on my own.
- I worry I didn't do enough for my husband.
- I worry I won't find joy again.
- I worry about my personal safety and living alone.
- I worry I will always feel alone, even in a crowd.

Scripture Focus

1

*"My flesh and my heart may fail, but God
is the strength of my heart and my portion
forever."*
Psalms 73:26 (NIV)

Our physical bodies will fail, but if we put our entire trust into our faith, our spiritual heart will live forever.

Widow Story

" **K**ermit the Frog was right: it is NOT easy being green — or a widow. It is sad; it is scary; it is awkward. Most of those beloved friends who want and try so hard to be helpful and supportive are still walking in the normalcy of life — marriage, retirement, travel, and respite. They don't know, just as I did not know, how life feels and works when you are the only one to rely on for handling decisions, tasks, celebrations.

There is family, and I could not ask for better family support. There are those special friends who also want to help. But at the end of the day, these wonderful people go back to life and on many days, I feel like I return to a void. My role feels like I am a permanent "extra," not fitting into a "couples" world. How many restaurants set tables for three or five?

I don't want sympathy or pity, just understanding if I decline an invitation to a New Year's Eve celebration or dinner party. Sometimes I can suck it up and do it; sometimes I just can't. Things that I am worried about often swarm around in my head, waking me in the night, distracting me during the day. My husband would have asked me, "Is this going to matter in 100 years?"

What we focus on magnifies.

Scripture Focus

2

"Do not be anxious about anything, but in everything by prayer and supplication with thanksgiving let your requests be made known to God. And the peace of God, which surpasses all understanding, will guard your hearts and your minds in Christ Jesus. Finally, brothers, whatever is true, whatever is honorable, whatever is just, whatever is pure, whatever is lovely, whatever is commendable, if there is any excellence, if there is anything worthy of praise, think about these things."
Philippians 4:6-8 (ESV)

When you are able, think about the things you are grateful for in life. It will remind you of all the great things God has given you and encourage you to live life to the fullest.

Widow Story

" **I**'m fine."

That has become my response when asked how I am after my husband passed.

Truth is ... I am not fine.

I am barely surviving, barely moving forward, barely making ends meet, barely keeping my sanity, and barely functioning.

"Barely" might not be the world's standard for success but in grief, it is enough. As long as I am making progress — even if it is barely — I will be okay.

Scripture Focus

3

"Surely he has borne our griefs and carried our sorrows; yet we esteemed him stricken, smitten by God, and afflicted."
Isaiah 53:4 (ESV)

We are not alone in our grief. Other widows have felt the same waves of sorrow we feel. Rely on and lean on others along your same journey.

Widow Story

"Being alone is hard — *really* hard. I was married for 44 years; being alone was temporary. I looked forward to aloneness to read or just be. The reason it was something to look forward to was because it was temporary. Now, it seems aloneness is a burden that gets heavier every day.

When I started writing this, I was feeling very sorry for myself. A friend was supposed to spend the day with me at the lake and she cancelled last minute. So, I'm at the lake by myself. I had just taken up a new hobby: paddle boarding. I'm not very good but I thought to myself, "What's the worst that can happen? I fall. If the waves get too big, I can paddle through them on my knees."

Don't be afraid to try new things. When our plans change, we have to make other choices. Happiness is a choice; being brave is a choice; doing something new is a choice. Start a new book. Take up a new hobby. Join a new group. We have to put ourselves out there, even when it's scary.

Instead of feeling depressed, now I feel I can do anything. The exercise was good for me; the solitude was actually nice, maybe because it was my choice to do something I enjoy — alone.

Scripture Focus

4

*"The Lord is my light and my salvation; whom
shall I fear? The Lord is the stronghold of my
life; of whom shall I be afraid?"*
Psalms 27:1 (ESV)

With the Lord on our side, we have nothing to fear. He is the light in our lives and our salvation.

Widow Story

"I have to do everything on my own now. It is overwhelming and scary. I have become a "don't know how" specialist.

I worry that when I do take the initiative to solve a problem on my own, I will make the wrong choice.

I try to focus on the scripture, "I can do all things through Christ." (Philippians 4:13 NKJV) It usually propels me forward; otherwise, I would become a statue and not move.

I have learned to ask for help. Many people want to help but don't know how. Reach out.

Worry: Reflection

_____
_____
_____
_____
_____
_____
_____
_____
_____
_____
_____
_____
_____
_____
_____
_____
_____
_____
_____
_____

– *Worry* –

_____
_____
_____
_____
_____
_____
_____
_____
_____
_____
_____
_____
_____
_____
_____
_____

*Thank you, God, for time with fellow travelers
in this journey. We lay our worries at your
feet. In the name of Jesus we pray, Amen.*

Courage

Meeting Opening Prayer

Mighty God, because of your faithfulness and love for me, I am discovering that with your help, I can do the hard things. I can do the scary things. I can try new things. I am growing into being a Philippians 4:13 woman. Because of you, I can be courageous. Thank you, Father, for the courage that trusting in You brings. In my Savior's name I pray, Amen.

Widow Voices

- I needed courage to move into another home.
- I needed the courage to deal with repairmen. I didn't want to get taken advantage of.
- I need courage to face isolation.
- It has taken courage to stand on my own.
- Every day brings new grief situations that I have to muster courage to face.
- I needed courage to take those first steps alone. Going to church, shopping, social and family events for the first time. Rebuilding a new life without your partner. Reaching that time of life you looked forward to sharing with that someone, only doing it alone.

Scripture Focus

1

"Have I not commanded you? Be strong and courageous. Do not be frightened, and do not be dismayed, for the Lord your God is with you wherever you go."
Joshua 1:9 (ESV)

God is not leaving your side. No matter where your grief journey takes you, He is with you.

Widow Story

"*I* was thinking about the things that my husband would never have believed I would be doing now. Partly because of my personality, partly because he spoiled me, and mostly because I never had to. Life these last few months has included leaving dishes in the sink, paying for help in establishing a flower bed, causing a huge television wall bracket to fall on my head, moving 90 miles away on my own, dealing with being stranded due to car issues, paying state and federal taxes before they were due, working through identity theft nightmares and bureaucracies that defy patience, and learning to follow my GPS to navigate new city destinations. It is not the boogie man that scares me. It is the technology fail — the sprinkler system malfunction, bills, repairs, lawn, not knowing my "purpose," and doubting my value moving forward. Each day is the same and yet new without my "partner." It is an *alone* that defies explanation and creates a hole I can't fill. And honestly, part of me does not want to fill the hole. I just want to crawl in it!

> "She continued to give her best, even when
> her best looked different from one season to
> the next."
> Morgan Harper Nichols

Scripture Focus

2

"I have fought the good fight, I have finished the race, I have kept the faith. Henceforth, there is laid up for me the crown of righteousness, which the Lord, the righteous judge, will award to me on that Day, and not only to me but also to all who have loved his appearing."
2 Timothy 4:7-8 (ESV)

There is no right way to grieve. We are all on the same journey, but each of us has a different path. Grieve how you want, rely on help from loved ones, and ask for God's assistance.

Widow Story

" My emotions change as I travel through my grief journey. They wane and can be difficult for me to express. They can be at the forefront and all I can do is cry, or they flip-flop at the drop of a hat.

Sometimes I feel as if I am on a rollercoaster ride, and I can't get off. I am making progress as I climb the steep hill; I even out and my path seems straight, then all of a sudden, I plunge into a depression that I find hard to climb out of.

I have learned that if I take time with God each day and focus on His grace, I can give myself grace and find the courage needed on my grief journey.

Scripture Focus

3

"When I am afraid, I put my trust in you."
Psalm 56:3 (NIV)

Don't let fear cause you to flee from God. Fear will flee from you as you ask Christ to increase your faith. When you're afraid, trust in God.

Widow Story

"It takes courage to thrive on your grief journey. The road is scary, rough, long, and hard to navigate. As Christians, we don't take the journey without hope.

Friends and family give you positive words of encouragement. It doesn't work when people are walking in front of you, trying to lead you down the path they think is right.

There is no shortcut, no finish line, no end. Mountains turn into hills, and the journey becomes more bearable to walk.

Widow to widow — I encourage you to push yourself. Tears are never far, but neither is joy. Every day, look for something beautiful on your journey. Courage and hope to become a thriver comes from God.

Scripture Focus

4

*"Commit to the Lord whatever you do, and
He will establish your plans."
Proverbs 16:3 (NIV)*

Truly committing to the Lord, whatever you do, puts all the heavy lifting on God.

Widow Story

" No one told me how much courage I would need to be a widow. I didn't know that I would need to be brave just to continue living. I didn't realize that I would have to ask God for courage to get out of bed each day. I didn't know I would have to pray for an appetite to be able to eat well and take care of myself.

It is okay to need help dealing with the changes that come with being a widow. We need to ask for help so we can keep moving forward. There is no shame in taking small steps.

Courage: Reflection

_____
_____
_____
_____
_____
_____
_____
_____
_____
_____
_____
_____
_____
_____
_____
_____
_____
_____
_____
_____

_____

_____

_____

_____

_____

_____

_____

_____

_____

_____

_____

_____

_____

_____

*O Lord, restore me to wholeness and
strength for service in your kingdom.
In Jesus' name, Amen.*

Protection

Meeting Opening Prayer

Gracious God, when my husband died, I felt vulnerable and at risk. For decades, my husband had protected me in every sense of the word. When he was no longer here, I found myself wondering if I would ever feel safe again. What I discovered in a new way was that You always were and will always be the protector of Your people. Your protection is promised in scripture, and the reality of that promise comes to us in a variety of ways. Thank you, God, for the knowledge that we are always safe within Your arms. Gratefully we pray in Jesus' name, Amen.

Widow Voices

- I have no one to protect me. No one knows if I make it home each day.
- I need protection from my emotions. Sometimes things get blown out of proportion.
- I need protection from doubt and second-guessing everything.
- I need protection from scammers who thrive on taking advantage of widows.
- I need protection from the stupid things people say who have never experienced the loss of a spouse.
- I need protection from being pushed into decisions which benefit others but are not in my best interests.

Scripture Focus

1

"However, as it is written: 'What no eye has seen, what no ear has heard, and what no human mind has conceived' — the things God has prepared for those who love him."
1 Corinthians 2:9 (NIV)

Our blessed hope is in Christ and the wonders of our eternal future are hidden in Him.

Widow Story

"*O*f someone were to ask me, "What do you need protection from in this season of living as a widow?" I would not say living alone, snakes, horror movies, or heights — even though those things can be legitimate causes for distress. But I seek protection from *myself* — my guilt, my worries, my stress about those things I cannot control since my husband died. I've often thought about why I feel so vulnerable and in need of protection, even though I fiercely proclaim my independence. Life is different, of course, but the same issues that assail me have always been there. What is different is obvious: my "protector" husband is not here to handle all the things that might make this "princess" feel insecure.

God provided my earthly protector, but He was always the source of that protection. And now that my beloved husband is off duty, I am finding that God and I have a renewed and powerful connection. I am finding that I am, as always, being fully protected. I just have to remember to seek and accept the protection He provides. I don't think He wants me to feel guilty that I took so long to figure this out. He knows me and that I am doing the best I can each day.

Scripture Focus

2

"'Because he loves me,' says the Lord, 'I will rescue him; I will protect him, for he acknowledges my name. He will call on me, and I will answer him; I will be with him in trouble, I will deliver him and honor him. With long life I will satisfy him and show him my salvation.'"
Psalms 91: 14-16 (NIV)

In the difficulties of living, we might strive to survive on our own. We forget that what we need most — God's protection and the comfort of His presence — are freely available to those who love Him and walk under His covering.

Widow Story

"Did you ever play the blindfold game as a child? You are blindfolded and your friend leads you around. You have to trust them not to run you into a wall.

That is what grief feels like to me. I am blindfolded and I don't know where I am going. Some days, I try to lead myself and I inevitably run into a wall. Other days, I let God lead me. I don't know where He will lead me, but He knows the best path for me.

God will direct and protect our steps as we grieve, if we allow Him to lead us.

Scripture Focus

3

"Do not let your hearts be troubled. You believe in God; believe also in me. My Father's house has many rooms; if that were not so, would I have told you that I am going there to prepare a place for you? And if I go and prepare a place for you, I will come back and take you to be with me that you also may be where I am. You know the way to the place where I am going." Jesus answered, "I am the way and the truth and the life. No one comes to the Father except through me."
John 14:1-4, 6 (NIV)

*L*ife can be troublesome; and if not troublesome, then tedious. It is normal for us to look for what lends meaning to our lives and gives us satisfaction.

Widow Story

66 Some days I feel like I am failing to move forward on my grief journey. I am slowly learning that failure is only final if I quit. I refuse to let failure be final for me. I choose to see failure as a steppingstone.

"... for though the righteous fall seven times,
they rise again." (Proverbs 24:16 NIV)

When you stumble and feel that you have lost the gains you have made, get back up. God is on your side. You can get back up every time grief knocks you down. God will restore you and protect you.

Failure to move forward is only final if you quit.

Scripture Focus

4

*"Come to me, all you who are weary and
burdened, and I will give you rest."*
Matthew 11:28 (NIV)

*"God is our refuge and strength, a very pres-
ent help in trouble."*
Psalm 46:1 (ESV)

*O*ur God is a strong shelter and a rock of refuge in whom we can hide during the storms and difficulties of life. He is our tower of strength, our firm fortress, and our secure stronghold to whom we can run for protection and safety.

Widow Story

"God Sighting! Most days I feel like I'm treading water. Today, I felt I was submerging. We were experiencing a pandemic. I was suddenly raising kids on my own, forced to educate them at home, trying to keep a job to support us, and now a winter storm had frozen my pipes. My husband always took care of those things. I didn't think to run water. My kitchen pipes burst, and I didn't know what to do. I was told by a friend to turn off the water. I ran outside but didn't know how to turn it off. I couldn't do it anymore. I fell to the ground and cried. I told the Lord that I give up. I prayed for help.

Just then, I heard a man's voice asking me if I was okay. I looked up to find a serviceman with a local plumbing company headed to a service call. He saw me on the ground and was concerned. He turned off my water, checked my house, and told me as soon as they finished their service call, they would be back.

God takes care of His widows!

Protection: Reflection

_____

_____

_____

_____

_____

_____

_____

_____

_____

_____

_____

_____

_____

_____

_____

_____

Father, this world can be a place of worry or a place of faith in your protection. Help us to choose the safety of your embrace. We love you. Thank you for loving us first! We pray in Jesus' name, Amen.

To learn more about Balcony Women,
visit www.balconywomen.com.

Balcony Women
Lifting Each Other Up In Love

Bringing new adventures to life, one word at a time.

www.designvaultpress.com

Made in the USA
Columbia, SC
07 August 2022

64822871R00102